DAILY LIFE
AROUND THE WORLD

by Katherine Talmadge Sallé

Table of Contents

INTRODUCTION

L et's visit three communities. They are in different parts of the world. We'll see how they are alike and how they are different.

First, let's go to a plains community in Africa. Plains are large, grassy areas. The Masai (mah-SY) people live there. They keep large herds of cows.

Next, we'll go to a river community in Cambodia (kam-BOH-dee-uh). Cambodia is in Asia. The Khmer (KMEER) people live there. We'll see families working together to grow rice and catch fish.

Finally, we'll go to Australia. We'll go to the **outback**. This is a large, dry plain. It is in the middle of the country. In the outback, we'll visit the town of Coober Pedy (KOO-buhr PEE-dee). There, many men work in mines. They dig for fine jewels called **opals** (OH-puhlz).

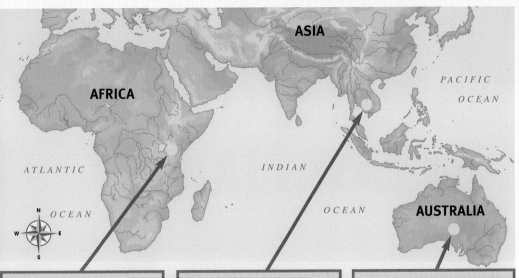

ASIA

AFRICA

PACIFIC
OCEAN

ATLANTIC

INDIAN

N
W   E
S

OCEAN

OCEAN

AUSTRALIA

Here is East Africa, where the Masai people live.

Here is Cambodia. Many small villages lie along the Mekong (MAY-kong) River.

Here is the mining town of Coober Pedy in the outback of Australia.

▲ The Masai move their herds from place to place on the plains of Kenya and Tanzania.

▲ In Cambodia, when the rice is ready to be picked, the whole family helps.

▲ In Australia, miners dig deep into the ground, searching for opals.

A PLAINS COMMUNITY IN EAST AFRICA

The Masai live in East Africa. They live on grassy plains and hot, dry deserts. There is little rain, so they do not farm. Instead, they herd. They take care of many cows. Cows are very important to the Masai. They even use cows as money.

▲ The Masai live in East Africa in Tanzania and Kenya.

▲ Most Masai wear **nanga** (NUHN-guh), loose-fitting robes that they tie at the shoulder. They do not wear shoes.

▲ Every time they move, the Masai must build new villages.

The cows need grass and water. That means the Masai can't stay in one place for long. When the grass is gone or the streams dry up, they must move. They are **nomads** (NOH-mahds), people who move from place to place.

THE VILLAGE

Each time the Masai move, they build a small village. It is called a **kraal** (KRAHL). All the men and women work together to build the village. The men build a high fence around it. The fence keeps the people and cows safe from lions and other dangerous animals. The women build huts out of sticks, grass, and mud. A hut has one big room with no windows.

A JOB FOR EVERYONE

In a Masai community, everyone works. Young children herd the calves. They have heard stories from the older people, so they know what to do. The children must work together to keep the calves safe from lions and hyenas.

Boys become men at twelve years old. They work together to search for grass and water for the cows. They might walk as many as thirty miles (forty-eight kilometers) in a day. Grown men are **elders**. They make the rules for the community. They decide when it is time to move.

Women and girls care for the huts, find water, and milk the cows. Everyone takes care of the cows.

ᐁᐁᐁ HISTORICAL PERSPECTIVE ᐁᐁᐁ

▲ Masai warriors wear their hair long.

The Masai believe that hair shows power or force. Most shave their heads to appear peaceful. But warriors must look forceful. So they grow their hair long. When men become elders, they must look wise and peaceful. So they cut their long hair. However, today the Masai living outside of East Africa wear their hair in many different styles.

VALUES AND CUSTOMS

Old Masai legends say that a god gave them cows. The Masai do not use money. Instead, they trade cows. Cows provide the Masai with food and drink. Many think the blood of a cow gives them strength.

PRIMARY SOURCE

"Cows are our way of life. They give us milk and blood and sometimes meat to eat and hides to wear. They're our wealth."

—Joseph Lemasolai Lekuton, Masai man

Masai women work with colored beads and a paint made from **ocher** (OH-kuhr), a brown clay. They make beautiful necklaces with the beads. Each color has a different meaning.

▲ Masai warriors paint their faces and dye their hair. The color red stands for blood and strength.

SCHOOL

Today, Masai boys and girls go to school. Since the Masai move with their cows, it can be hard for children to go every day. Some children stay behind and live at their school while their families travel with their herds.

Traditions (truh-DIH-shuhnz) are very important to the Masai. Traditions are customs and beliefs passed down from parents to children. In school, the children learn about how the Masai lived in the past. They learn Masai stories, legends, and tales. They also learn dances and songs. This helps them keep the past alive.

▲ a Masai school

They Made a Difference

Joseph Lemasolai Lekuton grew up in a Masai village. He was the only one in his village to go to school. He is now a teacher in Virginia. But each year, he returns to his village. He takes many of his eighth-grade students and their families with him. Once there, Mr. Lekuton, his students, and their parents try to live like the Masai. They wear Masai clothes, paint their faces, and herd cows. They also help build and repair schools.

During the school year, the students sell candy to raise money for the Masai school. They write to the Masai students. Then the American students and their parents travel to Africa. They buy cows for the school and its village. They meet their pen pals. They play soccer and have a lot of fun. They prove the truth in this Masai saying: "The mountains can never meet, but people can always meet."

✔ POINT

Think About It
Why do you think Mr. Lekuton takes his students to visit the Masai each year?

A RIVER COMMUNITY IN CAMBODIA

Let's go to Cambodia and visit a river community. The village lies along the banks of the Mekong River. That is the main river in Cambodia. It is a good place to farm and fish.

▲ The Khmer depend on the Mekong River. It gives them rich soil for their farms. It gives them fish, too.

About 200 Khmer people live in this small community. Most families grow rice and fish. Some also keep hens and pigs. Each member of the family goes fishing.

▲ The whole family works in the rice paddies. Rice is the most important part of the Cambodian diet.

MONSOONS, FLOODS, AND RICE PADDIES

Cambodia has two seasons. Each is caused by strong winds, called **monsoons** (mahn-SOONZ). From October to April, dry winds blow from the north. They bring dry weather. There is little rain.

In May, the wet season starts. Hot, wet winds blow in from the south across the sea. They bring heavy rain that falls for months. The Mekong River floods. Water and rich soil flow over its banks. This **irrigates** (EER-ih-gayts), or moistens, the fields. **Rice paddies** form. They are wet fields where rice grows.

▲ When Cambodians greet each other, they place their hands together and bow.

HISTORICAL PERSPECTIVE

Long ago, kings ruled Cambodia. At the courts, the people spoke French. But the village people spoke Khmer. Today, all the people speak Khmer. Children learn English in school.

FARMING

In July, farmers plant rice. Then they **harvest**, or pick, it in November. The whole family helps. They store the rice in big bags. They hope that the rice they grow will feed them for a year.

FISHING

Every family in a river community fishes. They use long, narrow boats. The boats look like rowboats. The people catch the fish with long nets. The men and women in the village make the nets.

Ponds form in the wet season. Fish are trapped there. Children catch the fish with their hands.

▲ Once people catch the fish, they salt it to preserve it. Cambodians eat fish raw, salted, and cooked.

AT HOME

Houses are built out of **bamboo**, a tall woody grass. Most homes have one large room. The families eat and entertain in that room. In the

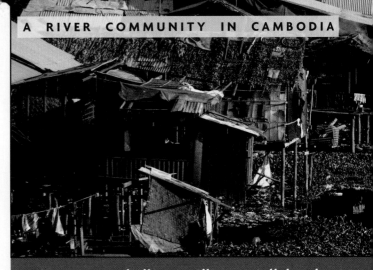

▲ Houses are built on stilts, or tall log legs. This keeps them dry during the yearly flood. It also protects the families from deadly snakes.

back are small bedrooms. The beds are mats made from straw.

Bathrooms are in separate buildings, called outhouses. The houses do not have running water. So people wash and bathe in the river.

AT SCHOOL

Khmer children go to school in their village. Since many villages do not have electricity, the schools use solar panels. The panels run computers and lights by using the sun's power.

It's a Fact

Grass houses can easily catch fire. So cooking is done in a shed away from the house.

The Khmer children learn math and science, as well as Cambodian traditions, legends, and history.

AN OUTBACK COMMUNITY IN AUSTRALIA

The outback is in the middle of Australia. It is a hot, dry desert. It has only five inches (13 centimeters) of rain each year. There are just a few trees, and there is no grass. Few people live there.

But there is an interesting community in the outback. It is called Coober Pedy. It is a mining community. People there mine opals. Opals are jewels.

▲ Australia is in the Southern Hemisphere, just south of the equator. That means its seasons are the opposite of ours. It's summer in December and winter in July.

OPALS ARE FOUND

In the 1900s, there was a gold rush in Australia. Willie Hutchinson and his father raced to the outback to find gold. They did not find gold, but Willie did find something valuable. He found opals.

Soon people heard about young Willie's opals. From all over the world, they rushed to the desert. They hoped to find more opals. They hoped to get rich. Very few did, but today many opal mines are worked there.

▲ Opals can be white, black, or bright blue. Often opals have specks of other colors in them, such as red, green, or yellow.

HISTORICAL PERSPECTIVE

Aborigines (a-buh-RIHJ-uh-neez) are Australia's native people. They live in the outback. They were surprised when white men came to the Coober Pedy area to dig for opals. The Aborigines thought the men were silly. They called such silliness *kupa piti* (KOO-pah PEE-tee). That meant "white men in a hole." Over the years, the name changed. Now it's Coober Pedy. Today, mining opals is a big business in Australia.

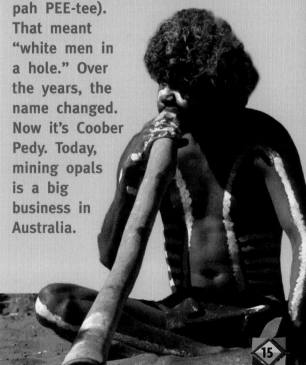

THE OPAL MINES

Miners must dig deep underground to find the opals. The hole, or shaft, might be 100 feet (30 meters) deep. Long ago, miners dug using picks and shovels. Today, they use machines.

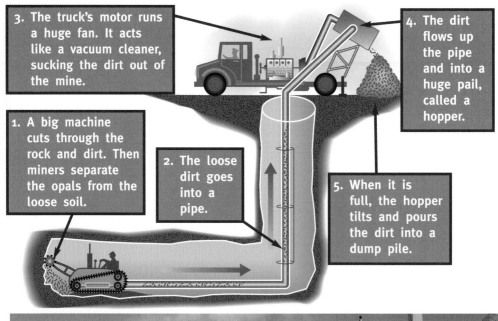

3. The truck's motor runs a huge fan. It acts like a vacuum cleaner, sucking the dirt out of the mine.

4. The dirt flows up the pipe and into a huge pail, called a hopper.

1. A big machine cuts through the rock and dirt. Then miners separate the opals from the loose soil.

2. The loose dirt goes into a pipe.

5. When it is full, the hopper tilts and pours the dirt into a dump pile.

▲ Most opals today are mined by individual miners, not companies.

Dump piles from the mines cover the sandy plains of Coober Pedy. These "dumps" bring in many tourists. They like to come here to "noodle." That is, they sift through the dump piles. They look for opals that the miners missed. Some people have been lucky. They've found opals worth thousands of dollars.

But opals are not the only special thing about Coober Pedy. The homes there are also different.

▲ Maybe these people will become lucky noodlers!

Almost 100% of the world's finest opals come from Australia. The sale of opals produced over $100 million in 1997. That's a lot of opals—and a lot of money!

▲ The dump piles look like giant anthills.

LIVING IN COOBER PEDY

It is very hot in Coober Pedy. In the summer, it gets up to 113°F (45°C). How do people beat the heat? Most live underground!

Their homes are called **dugouts**. Builders use big machines to dig tunnels into hills. Then they carve out rooms. Most rooms have windows, so there is a lot of light and air. The walls are packed dirt, with tan and red streaks. The floors are made of tile. Some of these homes even have underground swimming pools.

It's a Fact

Many people find opals when they are having their house dug. The families then sell the opals to help pay for their house.

▲ The temperature in the house stays comfortable, whether it's a hot day or a cold desert night.

▲ In Coober Pedy, the school year starts in January and runs until December.

AT SCHOOL

The school in Coober Pedy is not a dugout. It is like other schools except for one thing. It has its own radio station. The students help run the radio station. Many different languages are spoken in Coober Pedy. The radio station tells about events in the community in different languages.

The students also play many sports. A favorite is ice hockey! The students play ice hockey on rinks underground where the ice stays frozen.

COOBER PEDY AND THE MOVIES

Many people in Coober Pedy work in the mines. Others work in the tourist business. They run restaurants, hotels, and shops. Many of these places are underground, too. But there is another reason that people come to Coober Pedy.

People come here to make movies. Many of these movies are about other planets. The outback looks like what people think another planet, such as Mars, might look like. The ground around Coober Pedy is red, and Mars is called the red planet.

✔ POINT

Reread
Reread pages 19–20. Name three types of buildings you might find underground in Coober Pedy.

CONCLUSION

Look at a globe. Find where you live. Then find the three communities that we visited. They are many miles apart. Think about how these three communities are alike and different.

Each community is in a different part of the world. The land is different. One is near mountains and rivers, one is in a desert, and one is on grassy plains. The climates are different, and the homes look different.

But many things are the same. Families live and work together. Children go to school. While the communities are different in many ways, they also share a lot. Look at the chart on page 22 to see how these three communities are alike and different.

A Plains Community in East Africa	A River Community in Cambodia	An Outback Community in Australia

A Plains Community in East Africa

- grassy plains
- dry, hot climate
- huts made of sticks and wet dirt
- herds of cows
- small village, few people
- children live at school

A River Community in Cambodia

- Mekong River
- wet rice paddies
- small streams and ponds for fishing
- huts made of bamboo
- wet and dry climate
- small village, few people
- children go to village school

An Outback Community in Australia

- dry desert
- dry, hot climate
- underground "dugout" homes
- opal mines
- small town, few people
- children go to town school

GLOSSARY

bamboo	(bam-BOO) a tall, woody grass (page 13)
dugout	(DUHG-owt) an underground home (page 18)
elder	(EHL-duhr) an adult who makes decisions for a group of people (page 6)
harvest	(HAR-vihst) to pick a crop when it is ripe (page 12)
irrigate	(EER-ih-gayt) to supply land with water through streams, channels, or pipes (page 11)
kraal	(KRAHL) a fenced village of huts (page 5)
monsoon	(mahn-SOON) a seasonal wind that changes the weather in a region (page 11)
nanga	(NUHN-guh) a loose-fitting robe (page 4)
nomad	(NOH-mahd) a member of a group or tribe that does not have a permanent home but wanders from place to place (page 5)
ocher	(OH-kuhr) a brown clay used to make paint (page 7)
opal	(OH-puhl) a beautiful and costly gem (page 3)
outback	(OWT-bahk) a large, dry plain, or desert, that stretches throughout the middle of Australia (page 3)
rice paddy	(RYS PAH-dee) a wet, low-lying field where rice is grown (page 11)
tradition	(truh-DIH-shuhn) the practice of passing down customs, beliefs, or other knowledge from parents to their children (page 8)

INDEX